Canaries

Cliff Newby

Posters: a—Buff Norwich; **b**—New-color canary family; **c**—Buff Frill (photos by Harry V. Lacey).

Illustrations: Courtesy of Kosmos Verlag, 60. Harry V. Lacey, 17, 18, 19, 20, 21, 23, 57, 59, 61, 62, 64. Richard Smithers, 55, 56, 66, 78. R. A. Vowles, 4, 15, 16, 27, 28, 71, 79.

Back cover photographs courtesy of Vogelpark Walsrode.

This book previously appeared as *Canaries for Pleasure and Profit*. This new T.F.H. edition incorporates additional text and has been enhanced with new color photographs.

Distributed in the UNITED STATES by T.F.H. Publications, Inc., 211 West Sylvania Avenue, Neptune City, NJ 07753; in CANADA by H & L Pet Supplies Inc., 27 Kingston Crescent, Kitchener, Ontario N2B 2T6; Rolf C. Hagen Ltd., 3225 Sartelon Street, Montreal 382 Quebec; in ENGLAND by T.F.H. Publications Limited, 4 Kier Park, Ascot, Berkshire SL5 7DS; in AUSTRALIA AND THE SOUTH PACIFIC by T.F.H. (Australia) Pty. Ltd., Box 149, Brookvale 2100 N.S.W., Australia; in NEW ZEALAND by Ross Haines & Son, Ltd., 18 Monmouth Street, Grey Lynn, Auckland 2 New Zealand; in SINGAPORE AND MALAYSIA by MPH Distributors (S) Pte., Ltd., 601 Sims Drive, # 03/07/21, Singapore 1438; in the PHILIPPINES by Bio-Research, 5 Lippay Street, San Lorenzo Village, Makati Rizal; in SOUTH AFRICA by Multipet Pty. Ltd., 30 Turners Avenue, Durban 4001. Published by T.F.H. Publications Inc., Ltd. the British Crown Colony of Hong Kong.

Contents

The markings of the wild canary are exaggerated on the Lizard canary.

History of the Canary

In preparing this book, the author has sincerely attempted to cover thoroughly the proper systems of feeding, breeding, and managing canaries. He has also briefly described the early and authentic history of the canary and explained the most popular varieties in the numerous breeds.

History shows that the canary has been a favorite household pet since the year 1610; many of the present breeds were known as long ago as 1790, and more than twenty-eight different breeds of canaries have been bred during the last 348 years.

So, the canary is a long-established and well-domesticated song bird, and with each succeeding year it is becoming increasingly popular in almost every country in the world.

In the following pages, you will find sections on two of the newest members of the canary family: Red-factors, and the Red-factor—Borders. The former have in recent years become America's most fashionable show canaries, and the latter breed is rapidly catching on in popularity.

Lately, the Gloster canary which originated in England some years ago is becoming well known in America and is seen at the shows. The type canaries, such as Norwich, Yorkshire, and Border, have also made rapid strides in popularity here, and I predict that during the next few years their increase in the U.S.A. will be enormous.

You will find here, also, descriptions of cages and birdroom accessories. Bird seeds and other foods have been described in detail, and the famous artist R. A. Vowles and other illustrators have rendered some excellent pictures of canaries and many of the various articles used in canary keeping and breeding.

While the author has been most careful to cater fully to the requirements of beginners in the canary fancy, he also hopes the contents will be enjoyed by all bird fanciers and canary keepers in general.

The Canary Islands

Early canary history indicates that about 500 years ago a ship sailed from Spain, bound for Africa, but this boat never reached its destination, being wrecked on the rocky coast of the Canary Islands, which are located off the northwest coast of Africa. It is said that most of the sailors from this ship-wrecked vessel made their way to shore safely and remained on the islands for some time before being rescued.

Most sailors love pets, particularly birds, and it was not long before they discovered that their island of refuge was inhabited by birds they had never seen before and which had a most glorious song. During the temporary stay on the islands, the sailors began to observe these fine songsters closely. The males were bright green in color, the females a lightish gray green. They noticed they were seed eaters and were, therefore, members of the finch family. The birds, rather small in size, flew about in groups near the ground and fed on the seeding grasses which grew in abundance on the islands.

The irresistible song of these birds caused the ship-wrecked sailors to capture some of them.

They placed them in little cages fashioned out of thin twigs and bound together with long grasses.

The birds were lively and full of song, and their beautiful notes were so different from those of the birds of their native Spain that the sailors took home many of these songsters. Naturally, at first only the wealthiest people could afford to buy one of these lovely songsters; but, because of their rare singing ability, canaries gradually became the most popular song birds in Europe, and their fame as singers spread slowly to other parts of the world. While the canary is a fairly ancient bird, it was not by any means the first one kept in captivity. Before the canary was discovered, many other birds were enjoyed as pets; but, while they were most interesting, most of them lacked the fine song of the canary and were difficult to feed and keep in cages.

The King of Songsters

The canary has really earned the title "the king of the songsters," and it is recognized

History of the Canary

as such everywhere. It has become the most popular song bird in the world due to its unrivalled singing ability and because it is very easy to feed and care for—the canary actually thrives in captivity. The original canary was, of course, entirely different from those of today. It was smaller and not as attractive in color—a diamond in the rough, as it were, but an ideal cage bird.

How Breeding Improved the Canary

It took years of selective breeding to produce an all-yellow canary. No one person can be credited with accomplishing this miracle, but slowly the grass green feathers on many of the birds were bred out, and the pure yellow, or clear, canary was the reward for painstaking efforts of several breeders in Europe. The lighter yellow color made the canary more attractive to many, and the brightness of this color is more pleasing and vivid than most of the yellow found on other wild birds.

Today, a few breeders have produced, after years of effort, a canary that is quite close to red in color; in fact, these birds are actually light red. More about these lovely birds and how they were produced will be found in another chapter. They are called Red-factor canaries.

Many Types of Popular Canaries

Canaries can be divided roughly into two classes: song canaries and type canaries. The former are chiefly bred for their beautiful song, and the latter, because of their stately shape and size, are called "type birds" by fanciers. However, many of the large type birds are fine songsters, too, for those who like the "chopper" song.

Song canaries consist of Choppers and Rollers. The Choppers are loud singers and sing with their beaks wide open; the best of Rollers sing with their beaks nearly closed. Terms such as "St. Andreasburg" and "Harz Mountain" are names of places where canaries have been bred extensively; names such as "Golden Opera Singers" and other fancy terms are merely trade names.

Probably the most popular singing canary is the Chopper. This bird sings a rousing and cheery song in a rather boisterous fashion. The words *chop, chop, chop* can be heard clearly, hence the name Chopper. This breed of canary is the least expensive to buy and is probably the most widely bred of any canary. The song is natural and pleasing, even though it is loud in most specimens.

The Roller canary is a very soft and mild singer, not nearly as loud as the Chopper. It is a product of many decades of breeding for song only, although lately both better color and type are being bred into Rollers without destroying their splendid song. The Roller song consists of beautifully rendered notes, called rolls and tours. Among the notes the best specimens sing are: bass, hollow roll, flute, gluck, schockel, deep bubbling water tour, and several other pleasant notes. I am omitting mention of bell tours, because in my opinion, the best gluck rollers do not render any bell notes in their song.

Before you buy a bird, I suggest that you listen to several breeds of canaries. Ask your dealer or breeder to show you Rollers as well as Choppers. Also, listen to some of the type birds singing. In this way you can select just the bird whose song or beauty, or both, you prefer. It will also be greatly to your advantage if you can visit a bird show. They are held in the fall of the year in many cities. There you will see every breed of canary, hear every type of song, and see all the different colors, shapes, and sizes of the various birds.

Where Did the Different Breeds Originate?

Generally speaking, Germany produced the first Rollers and other song canaries. Fine singing canaries were also produced early in Belgium, Holland, Italy, Switzerland, and a few other European countries.

The British Isles are generally

History of the Canary

given credit for first producing the large, stately type birds, such as Norwich, Yorkshire, Lancashire Coppy, London Fancy, Scots Fancy, Lizard, Border Fancy, and Gloster. The United States has produced the American Singer and has probably made more headway with the Red-factor breed than other countries.

Some of the canary breeds, such as the London Fancy, Lancashire Coppy, Scots Fancy, etc., are nearly extinct today.

The British Isles has also produced some fine singing Roller Canaries such as Gluck Rollers. Their rich notes are very difficult to keep pure in young birds, but when properly rendered, they are beautiful. Gluck birds have more variety in their song than non-Gluck breeds, called Seiferts.

Another type of canary is the Dutch Frill, a rather peculiar bird, with some of its feathers loose rather than compact and close to the body as in other birds. The Netherlands produced the Dutch Frill and still breeds these unique canaries. Holland's fanciers also breed Red-factors

and other canaries and export them in large numbers—many to the U.S.A. The Scots and Belgian Fancy are also rather freakish hump-backed birds, which, when in position on the perch, hold their heads down and their shoulders up.

When it is considered that all these different breeds of canaries have been evolved from the original wild canary, great credit should be given canary breeders.

Who First Marketed Canaries on a Large Scale?

Germany was probably the first country to commercialize canaries in a big way, sometimes exporting them in lots of a hundred, a thousand, or even more, to just one customer. And, as they had hundreds of clients all over the world during the years since their first shipment, it is easy to understand that millions of canaries have been exported from Germany over the years, caged in little wicker cages. These were very small birds and were the least expensive of any on the market

9

History of the Canary

at the time. Later, when wars made the exportation of canaries from Germany difficult, American breeders really awakened and now produce probably finer birds, on the whole, than Europe does.

Everyone Should Own a Canary!

It has been rightly said that the canary is the only pet that sings. All children at an early age should be taught to care for a pet, and no pet is easier or more pleasant to care for than a canary. Grown-ups of all ages also find great pleasure in possessing a fine songster or two. Elderly people, shut-ins, and patients in hospitals will all find life more enjoyable if they share it with a canary. Persons who have retired should have a hobby, and there is no greater life-giving tonic in the world than the pleasure they can get every day of the year from keeping a canary.

Many nervous people have been completely cured after caring for a canary for a few months. The keeping of birds makes one forget his own troubles, for he thinks more of his birds than of himself. Handicapped people can often make themselves self-supporting by breeding canaries. Inmates of our prisons and mental institutions have been made fit to return to society again after having cared for canaries. I am glad to learn that many of our leading doctors are now recommending the keeping of canaries to many patients. They can be kept anywhere, by anyone. Often in our larger cities most pets are forbidden by property owners, but it is not likely that restrictions have ever been placed anywhere against keeping such an unobtrusive pet as a canary.

Working men such as miners, mechanics, and factory workers led the way in making canaries popular. Now, men, women, and children in all walks of life are keeping birds. Fine birds can be purchased everywhere, at popular prices, and the yearly cost of keeping a singing canary in one's home is lower than that of keeping most other pets.

The Different Breeds

The Chopper is probably the best known of all the different breeds of canaries. It is the bird usually kept as a house pet. Smaller in size than the type canaries, the chopper is ideal for one of the many styles of decorative wire cages seen in so many homes. The Chopper is hardy; a free singer; easy to care for; bred in various colors such as solid yellow, buff green, gray blue, cinnamon, white, and fawn. Some have dark markings; that is, they are partly yellow or buff with variegations of some of the other colors. The Chopper sings a loud, natural type of song.

The Roller

As mentioned before, the Roller is usually bred for song only, and up to a few years ago the best singers were generally solid green in color. Lately they have been bred in yellow, white, buff, orange, many other solid colors, and also in variegated shades. Rollers are peculiar in one respect; they sing with their beaks almost closed. Their song has taken years to develop. The best birds sing on command, usually starting with a very deep bass, and then going into a hollow roll; after which comes flutes, gluck tours, schockel, bubbling water tours, and many other song variations. Rollers used in singing contests are trained to sing immediately upon facing the judges. They are awarded so many points for one tour, so many for another, etc. Good Rollers utter no chop notes and sing far more quietly than the Chopper does. The best Roller song is bred into the birds and is not entirely due to training.

Hear a Roller Sing!

For some strange reason, Roller canaries are often greatly misunderstood as singers by people who should know better. The claim has been made that only true lovers of the opera can enjoy the song of the Roller. The fact is that a good Roller sings better than any other breed of canary, or any other singing bird, for that matter. Those who claim they don't like Roller song have

The Different Breeds

in most cases never even heard one sing! Those who have like the song in ninety-nine percent of the cases. Long ago, Chopper canaries earned the title of "jazz singers." This slogan and their low price made them more popular in the public mind than the far superior Rollers. In my opinion, this is a grave injustice.

The writer enjoys rock-'n-roll as well as opera—but he believes that a born, well-trained singer, whether human or a bird, can sing better than one with no natural talent or training. Even our best rock-'n-roll singers have had a thorough musical education. If you want the best, all-around singer of the canary family, investigate the Roller and hear the song.

Training Rollers for Contests

This begins soon after the weaning of the young birds. It is important they be out of hearing of birds that sing Chopper notes or faulty Roller song. For best results, young Roller-contest prospects should be kept in a room by themselves. I have

seldom used a tutor Roller, but if an extra-good singer is available, keep him near the young pupils.

Place In Training Cages Early

Contest prospects should be placed in these cages immediately after they complete their baby molt—and some fanciers molt them in these training cages with excellent results. Arranged in teams of four, one in each cage, and placed in the training cabinets which usually hold four cages, they are ready to begin training. At this time, the cabinet doors should be almost closed, and in the semidarkness the youngsters will be more attentive to their song development and not be too boisterous when learning and practicing their song. Keep them in semidarkness for a few weeks, opening the cabinet doors for 20-minute periods three times during the daytime and twice at night.

The next stage is to gradually darken the cages even more by closing the cabinet doors almost completely, and in a week or two your young Rollers are kept in total darkness, except for six

The Different Breeds

15-minute periods daily: three during the daytime and three at night. Rollers, of course, soon learn to eat and drink in the darkness. Keeping young Rollers in total darkness may seem cruel to the uninformed, but remember, this is just a training period and extends only a few weeks. It is their voice-tutoring time. While the song is bred into them, it must be practiced—the more the better, for their song development. After the twittering stage is past, the young Rollers slowly begin to render the adult song of pleasing, softly sung rolls, tours, etc. Keeping them in the dark makes them concentrate on their song practice, since there is nothing to distract them. They hear each other practicing, and each trainee follows suit trying to excel the others in singing freely.

So, by all means train young Rollers or American Singers in darkness. Allow them fifteen-minute light periods daily, plus an hour or two with facilities for bathing in flight cages once weekly. This will result in your birds obtaining better song training and learning to sing immediately when they are placed in the light.

One cannot blame the Roller judge for placing a No Song note on the tag of a cage containing a Roller which won't sing within about fifteen minutes in a singing contest. Personally, I have no use for a Roller which doesn't sing within five minutes after its cage is opened and facing the judge. A properly trained Roller will sing almost immediately in a song contest. A good one will sing either in daylight or under artificial light at night. It will sing the moment it is exposed to the light—its cue.

I have owned Roller canaries which, despite being tossed about all day traveling on bumpy trains, arrived at their destinations at 10:30 p.m. and began to sing within thirty seconds after being exposed to artificial light in the show room. Four of my Rollers once traveled from Detroit to New York, and due to a mistake or carelessness of a freight mover, traveled all night in their cages upside down! Next morning, at Madison Square Garden, they won first prizes for their singing ability.

The Different Breeds

After The Contest Season

This is the time to place your Rollers in large flight cages and give them the same care as to other breeds. Then they will be in good condition for the breeding season in the spring.

At one time it was mistakenly thought that contest Roller canaries must spend all their time in small singing cages or their song would be ruined. This false notion also applied to Linnets and other birds used in singing contests. But happily for the birds, these practices were exposed and condemned as long as 35 years ago.

The American Singer

These birds are beautiful singers, rendering both Roller and Chopper song notes in what generally may be called a Warbler type of song. They are bred by crossing a Roller canary to a Border Fancy canary. Thus, their song is partly Roller and partly Chopper. They are raised in the many different colors described under Choppers. They are becoming very popular because their song, being of a Warbler type, is neither too loud, too soft, nor too harsh in tone. American Singers are beautiful and possess some of the fine type of the Border Fancy breed. The American Singer can be recommended very highly as a singer and pet.

Some day I predict the American Singer will replace the Chopper as a house pet, because this breed is bred by fanciers who place quality before quantity. Naturally, he costs a little more than a common Chopper. He is bred along pedigree lines. American Singers will live longer and be less expensive in the long run than the Choppers.

Those who desire to exhibit at the shows should train their American Singers the same as suggested for the training of young Rollers. It seems to me that many fail to sing freely because they were never properly trained.

The Red-factor Canary

The Red-factor is also a new breed and has rapidly become

The Different Breeds

one of the most wanted canaries. The colors of the best birds are very deep red orange (almost red), pink, apricot, red bronze, and copper. Their colors are natural, and these reddish tones were bred into the birds by crossing a male Red Siskin with a Border Fancy or Roller canary hen. Some of the offspring from this cross proved fertile, and later, when mated back to canaries, gradually produced beautiful birds of a deep red orange and other striking colors. The aim of the Red-factor breeder is to produce an all-red canary. Selective breeding may make this goal feasible. Red-factors usually sing a Warbler type of song, although some have been bred to render pure Roller notes. This breed, because of its natural richly colored beauty and fine song, will become a most popular house pet in time.

Fanciers who breed Red-factors must often wonder what miracle of nature really made it possible to propagate this breed. According to all laws of nature, reds should have been impossible in the first place. The Red Siskin male cross with the hen canary is

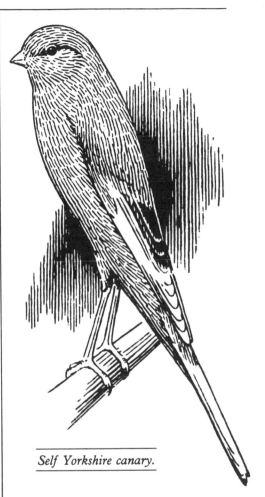

Self Yorkshire canary.

the first case and one of the rarest cases in bird history that I know of, where two different species of finches, the Red Siskin and the hen canary, when mated together, did produce certain fertile male offspring in the first cross.

The Different Breeds

Posture is the most significant characteristic of the Scots Fancy breed.

Let us examine this subject in another way. If we mate a male Linnet, Goldfinch, or some other similar hardbill to a hen canary, they will produce youngsters—but these are all sterile and remain so. We cannot breed any further with these birds. They are rightly called mules, named after the cross between a donkey and mare, also sterile.

When I think of all the hardbill finches which when mated to hen canaries produce only sterile youngsters, and then think of the lone South American siskins producing fertile males in their breeding with canary hens—only then do I realize what a miracle this really is!

Avoid a Five-Year Job

Instead of purchasing siskins and attempting to breed your

Photographs, pp. 17—24: 17—Colorfed Yorkshire canary cock. 18—Red-factor and Clear canaries. 19—Red-factor pair and nestlings. 20—Cinnamon Self Yorkshire. 21—Clear Border Fancy. 22—Hen feeding young. 23—Scots Fancy. 24—"Canary yellow" incarnated.

The Different Breeds

own strain of Red-factors by crossing male siskins with female canaries, I advise you to save years of effort, and possibly much disappointment, by obtaining top-notch red-factors that may be many years removed from the siskin-canary hybrids from which they were originally descended. There are some splendid "ready-made" Red-factors obtainable today. The deep colors are well set into them, and they will reproduce their own colors or even deeper ones in some cases. This will save you a lot of grief and at least five years' work, which you could spend more profitably and interestingly, in helping to produce a deep red canary.

Most Popular Canary on the Show Bench

The Red-factors, called New-colored canaries in England, are most fascinating to keep and breed, and are easily the most numerous canaries seen on the show bench in the United States. In some European countries also it is very, very popular as a show bird.

The deepest colored birds seen to date at the leading canary shows are about the color of a ripe tomato. I strongly urge novices to procure a few Red-factors, as they will prove to be one of the most interesting varieties in many ways. For instance, when breeding these birds, one never knows just what color the youngsters will develop into; some may be yellow, others light orange, and the most sought-for birds will be deep red orange. A few young birds, when first feathered, are pure white, molting out later into very deeply colored red orange or pink birds.

Sometimes the light orange birds, depending on their backgrounds, will produce very deep youngsters; but, as a general rule, I advise novices purchasing Red-factors to get only the very deepest birds that they can possibly find. Then their chances are much greater and surer in being able to breed really deep birds.

Sometimes the light orange birds, depending on their backgrounds, will produce very

The Different Breeds

deep youngsters; but, as a general rule, I advise novices purchasing Red-factors to get only the very deepest birds that they can possibly find. Then their chances are much greater and surer in being able to breed really deep birds.

Tomato-red birds are quite expensive, and the females, if really deep in color, cost just about as much as the males. As a general rule, Red-factor hens are never quite as deep in color as the deepest males; they seem to follow the pattern of several other breeds of canaries, the females usually being lighter in color than the males.

Frosts and Nonfrosts

The frosted birds, both males and females, show white tints on their feathers, giving the overall appearance of a light veil over the reddish ground tones of the birds. Some are more heavily frosted than others. Viewed in good natural light, preferably toward evening on a sunny day, many of the birds appear to be a distinct pink in color.

Frosted Birds Are Better in Type than Nonfrosted

The frosted Red-factors are nearly always better in type than the nonfrosted birds. The best are of fairly good Border type. This is due largely to their feather structure; the feathers are more compact and more thickly distributed over the birds. They are also usually less leggy than the nonfrosts because they show less thigh when in good position on the perch.

However, the nonfrosted Red-factor canaries have shown some amazing improvements in type during the last few years, and their feathers are less brittle than they once were. The mating of two nonfrosted birds together results in easily broken and fragile feathering on their youngsters. It is always better to mate a frost to a nonfrost, to follow out the good old rule of only mating a yellow to a buff, as it were.

Which Are Deeper in Color and Closer to Red?

Most people, unfamiliar with the Red-factor breed, think that

The Different Breeds

The Dutch Frill (above) is one of the breeds that exhibit unusual feathering, while unusual posture characterizes the Belgian (below).

the nonfrosted birds, which carry no white on the outside of their feathers, are deeper in color and closer to red than the frosted birds. But a close examination under a good magnifying glass shows that there is less yellow in the frosted birds than in the nonfrosted variety. Therefore, that section of their feathers not mixed with white is actually closer to red than that of the other birds. So, most experienced Red-factor fanciers and judges generally credit the best frosted birds with being closer to actual red than the nonfrosts, which have more visible yellow in their coloring, even though most of it is very deep red orange—something of a feathered optical illusion.

Always Mate Frost to Nonfrost or Vice Versa

Red-factor breeders have found that the mating of two frosted birds together produces only light-colored birds. And they have discovered that the mating of two nonfrosted birds with each other brings forth tiny, poorly shaped heads that many

The Different Breeds

Above: the canary crest figures mainly in two breeds: the Crested and the Gloster. Below: Scots Fancy.

fanciers have rightly named "snake-headed." Also, as mentioned above, the nonfrost mating produces thinly and poorly feathered specimens.

So, of course, the best possible mating for this breed is frost to nonfrost. It does not make any difference whether the male or female be the frosted bird.

Red-factors Are Easy to Breed

I have found that if properly fed, housed, and managed, this attractive variety is a most prolific breeder, fully as simple to breed as the popular Border Fancy canary. Red-factors are very active birds, always on the go when in a good state of health, and, when in proper breeding condition, they begin nesting eagerly. Both parents, I have found, are nearly always very good feeders. Their usual clutch of eggs is four, but sometimes five and even more eggs are found in their nests. I have never seen a destructive or mischievous male Red-factor. They have always been of great assistance to the hens when feeding youngsters, and I

The Different Breeds

strongly urge my readers who breed Red-factors to leave the breeding pairs together whenever possible.

The Dimorphic Hen

This chalk-white, lilylike bird with faint markings of orange or light red showed up first in Europe, about fifty years ago. Once you see one of these birds, you will never forget its appearance. It has a certain distinctiveness all its own. The pleasing and delicate color scheme is entirely different from all other canaries. Some specimens show dark markings—variegations, as it were—and some carry more tints of orange or light red than others. Dimorphic hens are also being produced with very distinct pink markings, which make them even more attractive than the orange- or light-red-marked birds. In my opinion, they are the glamorous beauties of canarydom. These hens are still fairly scarce, and because many fanciers believe they pass on certain desirable color

relationships of the Red Siskins, they are much in demand.

Occasionally, I talk to an experienced fancier who claims Dimorphics are not of much value in the breeding room, but my own experiences with them have been most encouraging. Mated to very, very deep nonfrosted males, a few nearly red canaries have been produced in both frosted and nonfrosted birds. But to breed these, really deep red-orange sires should be used.

It has also been my privilege to examine the pedigrees of some of the deepest Red-factors produced in America. Nearly always these have shown Dimorphic hens somewhere in the background fairly frequently, so I strongly urge the Red-factor breeder to possess one or two of these hens. But be sure you get a genuine Dimorphic, not a whitish-appearing ordinary canary.

Red-factor Hens Worth as Much as Cocks

Ask the average person and he will state that female canaries are

The Different Breeds

worth less than the males. Nothing could be further from the truth. Only in a few of the most common and least expensive breeds is this true. Due to their scarcity, Red-factor hens are very difficult to buy at any price, i.e., the very deeply colored ones. Only a very few hens out of each hundred Red-factors bred have as much color depth as the best cocks.

The Dimorphic Male

There are many recognized fanciers who still claim there are no Dimorphic males, as this dimorphism, they think, is strictly confined to the hens. For many years I heartily agreed with this belief. And then it was pointed out to me by a fellow fancier that some of my males were Dimorphics, and not long afterwards more and more Dimorphic birds appeared among my young canaries. The males are fairly easily recognized when one has had experience with them. They resemble the hens, but are more richly colored, as a rule.

All Dimorphic Canaries Are Frosted

In purchasing Dimorphics, especially males, buy only from a reliable source, as many ordinary whitish-appearing canaries are palmed off as genuine Dimorpics to the inexperienced. If at all possible, see the Dimorphics at a canary show. As said before, once you have seen one, you will always remember it.

Pinks Seem To Be in Front

Pink canaries are very rare and are produced from pink-strain birds only. There are two shades—frosted pink and nonfrosted pink. Nonfrosted pinks are very scarce indeed, and there are still many fanciers who claim that all pink canaries must be frosted. Pink canaries carry no visible yellow coloring; that is why their color is so beautiful and outstanding.

Red-factor–Borders

As the name implies, this is a cross between the Red-factor and

The Different Breeds

Border canaries, and is usually done with a view to improving type in the Red-factor. Red-factor–Borders are becoming increasingly popular at the shows, for they are a canary of striking beauty. As I have written many times, the fancier who really succeeds in producing a canary equal in size and type to the best Borders and is fortunate also in breeding this bird in a very deep red-orange color will possess a bird that will win many trophies and blue ribbons at the shows.

To date, I have never seen a Red-factor canary of very deep color that is as large, as well shaped, and as handsome as the best exhibition-type Borders one sees at the shows.

So this is a rewarding goal for all Red-factors breeders, and someone, someday, will succeed.

How to Breed for Best Results

Let us assume that you possess two of the very deepest near-red Red-factor males, and that they are in sound health, are of good size and shape for this breed, and are nonfrosted birds, which carry the deep color well into their wings and tail feathers. They must be of deepest color, and should be as non-leggy as possible.

To use only a light- or medium-deep bird for this cross would be a sheer waste of time and effort, as only lightly colored youngsters could appear from such a mating.

The next step is to procure two extra-large, exhibition quality, buff Border hens. If possible, buy two extra-large Border hens that have won first-prize ribbons at a good show, or get them from a Border breeder who has won a lot of prizes. They must be extra large and of standard type. They must be buff-colored hens, preferably clears, although some outstanding youngsters have been bred in this cross from ticked or lightly variegated Border hens and clear Red-factor males, or vice versa.

Mate the Border hens with the Red-factor males as you would other canaries, but bear in mind that the nest pans must be large to accommodate the Border hens, and their breeding cages should be the box type, and as big as those used in Yorkshire and Norwich breeding.

When the offspring from these Red-factor–Borders arrive, let them molt out, if possible, in a large flight cage. When the molt is well under way, you will note the respective colors of the birds. Some you will recognize as being buffs; others, the deeper-colored birds, as being nonbuffs. The best specimens will be of lovely Border type, and when the molt is finished, they will show about 50 percent of the color of the red-orange Red-factor males in the nonbuff specimens.

How to Proceed the Following Year

The next step, the following year, is to mate one of the deepest and best nonbuff males to his buff Border mother. In canary breeding, always employ the long-tried and well-proven principle of mating yellow to buff birds. If you raised a buff Red-factor–Border hen, you will then mate her to her deep red-orange Red-factor father. Do this

with the offspring from both pairs.

This will be a good way of getting your Red-factor–Border stud begun in good fashion, and in following years you will discontinue mating the birds back to their pure Border mothers and instead will mate them to your best Red-factor–Borders, occasionally going back to the pure Red-factor red-orange fathers to keep the color deep, and will continue a selective color-breeding program, always mating your best and deepest colored birds together and discarding the others.

Breed Closely If Necessary

By this I mean that it won't hurt to breed brother to sister, father to daughter, daughter to father, etc., occasionally; or you can mate other close relatives together to still further improve color and type. There is no harmful effect in doing this if your birds are all in sound health, but never breed close relatives with each other if they show the least signs of sickness or if the color and type of the birds are not good in every respect.

Use only your best-colored and most typey birds; eliminate all the others as breeders, and I believe that in time you will be well on you way to producing a deep red-orange Red-factor–Border.

I will state frankly here that there is no sure formula yet worked out for producing the red-orange Red-factor–Border; also there are other problems to be solved before this truly deep cross between the two breeds may be bred, but it is well worth anyone's effort to try for it, and all we can do at present is to work along the lines I have suggested here.

Those alert fanciers who like to get in on the ground floor of things will find it deeply interesting and possibly very profitable, too, to raise Red-factor–Border canaries. For these, in my opinion, are among the most beautiful canaries, and their popularity at all the big shows is jumping to the front fast. Yes, more and more fanciers are breeding Red-Factor-Borders,

and many write me asking where they can buy suitable Border hens to breed with Red-factor males. You will, I believe, learn that really typey Border hens are difficult to find because many prominent Border breeders have more males for sale than hens. If you can't buy one from a breeder, the best place to purchase a fine Border hen would be at a canary show.

Agate, or Dilute, Canaries

This is a distinct breed of canaries slowly becoming popular in the United States. Most of us understand that the word *dilute* in a color sense means to make paler and weaker a certain dark color. If we take black paint and mix white with it, the black loses strength in color depth and becomes lighter, diluted, as it were. This principle roughly illustrates the paleness of color found in the darker feathers of a marked or variegated dilute canary.

It must be remembered that this color-paleness, or pastel effect, occurs visibly only in the

The Different Breeds

darker feathers; the ground, or overall, color of the bird, whether it be yellow or Red-factor, is not changed. A clear bird may be of pure dilute ancestry, but will not show it.

The original dilute canary, a female, was first bred in Holland and was not a "sport" in the true sense; but it had the means of transferring the dilute color to some of its male offspring. The dilute colors are pale, pastel shades of all the normal dark variegated canary colors. Dilutes are also called agate canaries because their jewel-like blending of colors resembles certain of our semiprecious stones of the agate family.

Not many people understand that some dilute canaries carry a stronger visible color pigment than others, and should be divided into two classes; that is, dilutes showing maximum pigment and minimum.

A prominent Belgian canary judge once sent me four dilute canaries that he procured from a well-known breeder of these birds in Holland. They were all birds showing maximum color pigment. One of the males I entered in a dilute class at one of our leading shows. There he was called a nondilute and immediately reclassified and transferred! He was awarded first prize in the nondilute red-cinnamon class.

The Norwich

The Norwich, one of the largest of the type birds, was first bred in Norwich, England. It is well-rounded, nobby, and chubby in appearance and comes in many colors. Too large a bird to keep in a small, all-wire canary cage, it is best kept in a square, box-type cage at least eighteen inches wide by eighteen inches high. Some of the newer and larger wire or plastic cages are large enough for it. The Norwich is a fairly good singer of the Chopper song and is a tame and steady bird, although lazy in some respects. This breed ought to be an ideal one for those who like to teach canaries to do tricks, as it is fearless. Usually this variety is kept only by fanciers, but there is no reason why it should not become a popular house pet.

The Different Breeds

Crested Canaries

Similar in appearance to the Norwich canary, and coming in about the same colors, this breed has a large crest and appears in shades of buff, very deep yellow, green, cinnamon, and white. There are clear, ticked, and variegated colors. Some of the best birds have evenly marked contrasting darker feathers on wings, head, or both. Some have light crests and a dark body, others have a dark crest on a light body. A few of the white specimens show tinges of blue markings, but these are quite rare.

When breeding Crested canaries, never mate two crested birds together, because this has a tendency to spoil the even effect of the crest and to cause the appearance of other unwanted feather structures. Better to use a Crestbred, that is, a bird of this breed that has no crest. Both crested birds and noncrested ones, called Crestbreds, are produced from a Crested mated to a Crestbred. Unlike the Norwich, Crested canaries should not be color-fed.

The Yorkshire Canary

The Yorkshire is a large, tall, slim, and slender bird, the best being wedge-shaped. It was first produced in Yorkshire, England. Bold and military in appearance when standing "at attention," the Yorkshire is a fine sight to behold. It is bred in nearly all colors, including white, and is a very popular exhibition bird. The best specimens are quite expensive. The Yorkshire needs a large cage, such as for the Norwich canary. While kept mainly by keen fanciers, there is no reason why it should not be seen also in the home as a house pet, as it is a good Chopper singer and has stately appearance.

The Border Fancy

The Border Fancy was produced first in the British Isles, being bred most extensively on the border of England and Scotland, hence the name. The Border Fancy is now easily the most popular breed of canary in Great Britain. A little larger in

The Different Breeds

size than the Chopper and Roller breeds, it is a well-shaped and fairly chubby bird, with a well-rounded head, and large, bold eyes. It is similar in appearance to the Norwich canary, but smaller. Seeing one of these birds with its deep and rich natural yellow colorings, its perfectly carried wings, and tight glistening feathers, is something one never forgets. Besides being one of the most popular show canaries in the world, there is no reason why it should not be a more desirable house bird as well. He sings a nice, sweet Chopper song and comes in nearly all the canary colors.

The Gloster Canary

The Gloster canary is a comparatively new breed which originated in England. In general appearance, it resembles the Border Fancy canary, but has a neat, well-rounded crest, which covers about half the bird's eyes. It is a beautifully feathered breed and is already quite popular in England, and has become so here. The Gloster is ideal as a singing house pet, as well as a show bird.

The Lizard Canary

These birds are rightly named, for the feather coloring on their backs and shoulders are scale-shaped and resemble those of a lizard in appearance, but not texture. They are beautiful canaries and are bred in two colors: gold and silver. Because of their unusual appearance, they create quite a lot of interest at canary shows. They used to be bred extensively in England, then faded out of style for awhile, but are now coming back again very strongly in popularity.

The London Fancy

This breed is now nearly extinct, I am sorry to say, although it was most popular in the last century. These are very large birds, and some are beautifully and evenly marked in their feathering. The breeding of canaries with perfectly balanced and evenly marked darker

The Different Breeds

feathers is an art; such birds are very rare.

The Scots Fancy

The Scots Fancy is a product of Scotland. It is seldom seen except at canary shows, and then in very limited numbers. When standing in position, this strange canary holds its head down about one-third the length of its body, and its rounded shoulders jut upward like a mountain. In general appearance, the peculiar stance of this bird makes it appear hump-backed. It is bred mostly in yellow and buff colors. Because of their rarity and novel appearance, Scots Fancies are expensive.

The Dutch Frill

As its name suggests, this breed of canary is a product of Holland, and instead of the breast and some of its other feathers lying close to the body as in other birds, they actually turn upward and outward, giving it a rather frilly appearance. Dutch Frills are not common even in Holland, and are seldom seen except at canary exhibitions.

Linnet-Canary Mules

I could not end my description of the popular breeds of canaries without briefly mentioning these delightful birds. Linnet-canary mules were the first birds I bred as a boy. Had fine beginner's luck too—eight beautiful birds were reared from my one pair in two nests.

The Linnet is a most melodious songster to those who like wild-bird notes. Kept in a large box cage, fed good rape seed, canary, and a pinch of linseed once in a while, plus lots of wild seeds, seeding heads, and fresh green foods of all kinds, the Linnet soon becomes very tame, more so in fact than many canaries do, and will readily mate with a hen canary when both birds are in proper breeding condition.

The youngsters, especially those known as light mules, are beautiful birds; and the males, whether light or dark birds, are excellent songsters. Unfortunately, they are sterile.

What Breed Should I Buy?

As mentioned before, attend a canary show if possible, and see all the different varieties that are staged there. If you desire a canary as a house pet, you probably want a good singing breed such as a Chopper or Roller. But please bear in mind there are now available for your consideration several other excellent singing breeds, such as Red-factors, Border Fancies, American Singers, and others. Nowadays you can procure a beautifully shaped and colored canary that will sing most pleasingly. There is no need for you to purchase a bird for its singing ability alone. The best canaries combine beauty, type, and song. Some people, of course, prefer the softly singing Roller canary to the Chopper. Then there are those who will get only a loud singer, such as the Chopper. Happily for all concerned, there is a breed of canary to suit every taste and pocketbook, and our previous descriptions of the unlimited choice of varieties will give you an idea of what each breed is like.

When and How to Buy a Canary

After you have fairly well decided what breed of bird to procure, you should bear in mind that there are proper and improper times of the year to buy canaries. Don't buy one during the molting season. The natural molting time for canaries is between July and October. In northern areas, many birds do not begin molting until about August and are not completely finished until early in October, when they gradually come into full song. In southern regions, some canaries may finish molting long before this. However, as a general rule, it is safest to buy a canary during the period from October until February or March. Canaries are in best song during these months.

It is foolish to buy a canary while it is molting or about to go into a molt. Moving a bird from one home to another and giving it different food and treatment at this time is most likely to upset the canary and perhaps result in the death of your bird. Canaries you intend to use as breeders the

What Breed Should I Buy?

following year should never be purchased later than December if you want them to go to nest the following March or April. Always allow plenty of time for canaries to become accustomed to new surroundings.

Perhaps you may wonder where to purchase a canary. If you live in a large city, you will be able to get most of the popular breeds at pet shops or from a breeder. Also, you will find most of the different breeds advertised in pet and canary magazines. There is a bird club in almost every large city; inquire about it; its members will be more than pleased to give you dependable advice.

In most cases, and except in show birds, the females are usually worth much less than the males. You may rest assured that all canaries advertised as unsexed are females; there is not likely to be a single male among them.

What Age Canary?

Remember, you cannot be sure of any canary's age unless it wears a closed leg band which is put on the bird's leg at about eight days of age. Canaries are probably at their best as singers or breeders when they are from one to four years of age. As a general rule, I think it best to purchase a bird that is not over two years old. Canaries have been known to live for as long as fifteen years, but the average life span is about eight years. As canaries become older they usually show their age by a scaly leg condition. Avoid these birds.

Are Imported Canaries Better?

As a matter of fact, good canaries are raised in nearly every country. But it must be remembered that there is a big demand everywhere for the most outstanding birds, that is, the best specimens. So, it is usually not the finest birds that are exported, because the really good ones sell easily in their own countries. Birds exported from abroad are often poor specimens. If you desire to import canaries from foreign countries, use great caution. As a general rule, and

What Breed Should I Buy?

unless you are seeking some breed not obtainable in America, you are wise to purchase canaries bred in America. One raised in a foreign country is not used to our climate, our ways of feeding, etc.

When You First Get a Canary

Have a suitable cage ready. For a house singer, an all-metal or plastic cage made by a reliable manufacturer is all right. Avoid a too-fancy cage, as it is difficult to keep clean. The simpler and larger the cage, the better. It should be hung or placed, if on a stand, in a suitable space in your room, and its height from the floor should be no higher than your eye level. Even a lower position is often better, for at a height above your head, the temperature in a heated room is often far too high for a canary. The cage should never be hung or placed directly in front of windows. A suitable place at the side of a window is much better, as it will be free from drafts there. Avoid long exposure to direct sunlight, but occasionally your bird may enjoy a thirty-minute sunbath in moderate sunshine, and this is good for him; so move his cage to a sunny spot for a short period every now and then.

The temperature at the place where your bird's cage is permanently placed is most important. It should never be more than seventy degrees in winter. Higher temperatures may cause your bird to go into what is called a soft molt. Once this begins, it is difficult to stop. The more constant and uniform this heat, the better for the bird. If the temperature drops to fifty-five or sixty degrees during the night, it will not harm your bird. Actually sixty-five degrees is the best temperature for your canaries.

In summer during the hot weather, keep your bird's cage in as cool a place as possible. Sometimes in winter, your room thermostat may register a much lower temperature than it actually is at the spot where your cage is suspended, so check there with a thermometer. Avoid a hot spot for the cage, for that is the

b

What Breed Should I Buy?

worst of all places for it.

The bottom of a canary's cage can be covered with newspaper or special paper sold at pet shops. Then it will be easier to clean than if you used sand or gravel on the cage bottom. Change this paper every third day or so. Be sure to have a piece of cuttlebone fastened to the wires of the cage where the canary can reach it comfortably. This, along with a suitable bird sand, preferably placed in a small dish in a corner of the cage, is an absolute necessity. Gritty sand is like teeth to a bird, enabling it to digest its food via the gizzard. Also have a treat cup for the bird; this is made to fit securely between the cage wires.

Place seed and water in receptacles and a little treat seed in the treat cup. Now you are ready to place your bird in its cage. Put the bird in gently and avoid approaching the cage too closely at first, until he has had time to look around and become acquainted. If it is a young bird, it will usually be more timid at first than an older one. Be patient; it may take a few days for your canary to setle down,

and it might even take a few weeks if it has previously been kept in a large flight cage or aviary.

As a general rule, reliable pet shops and breeders do not directly sell canaries that have been flying loose in an aviary, but take them out for several weeks and keep them in individual cages prior to the time they dispose of them. They can then give you a much steadier and tamer canary.

Some canaries sing soon after you buy them, others do not begin for some time. The main idea is for you to gain your bird's confidence; at all times move very slowly and gently around his cage, especially when you are feeding him and cleaning the cage. As soon as the bird becomes used to his new surroundings, he will commence to sing. Very often, in the beginning, a new bird can be coaxed into singing by shaking a partly filled kitchen matchbox some distance away from the cage. The noise the large matches make rattling in the box seems to be enjoyed by canaries.

What Breed Should I Buy?

A Daily Schedule

Feed and water your canary every day. The water cup should be well scoured each day, using a detergent to make it sparkling clean. Any husks in the seed cup should be blown away and fresh seed added. If your canary at first eats only the white canary seed and avoids the dark rape seed, do not worry, but always make sure it always has the light-colored seed, as well as the dark, in the seed cup, because most adult canaries eat more of the light seed than the dark. Perches in your canary's cage should all be removed at least once a week and thoroughly scrubbed in hot, soapy water. The canary won't get rheumatism if you wash his perches instead of scraping them, as some people think. Washing the perches kills all germs that may be on them; mere scraping does not.

The best time for a canary to bathe is right after you clean his cage, because this is when he prefers to bathe most. Usually a canary will bathe more readily in an oval bath set on the cage floor—but if it can be induced to enter an outside bath, one that hangs outside of his cage door, so much the better. Often it takes some birds quite a while to get used to outside baths; they seem afraid of them. Sometimes if you place a little green food in the shallow water, it will help matters. In summer, canaries may be offered a bath every other day or so; in winter, twice a week is plenty. Never force a canary into the bath. If he won't bathe, don't worry; spray non-bathing birds with an atomizer, but do this only when the room is warm, and early in the morning.

Many birds are ruined because their thoughtless owners think they can stay awake late every night and remain in good health. Such is not the case. A canary needs more sleep than an adult human. He likes to go to sleep as soon as darkness falls, and his cage should be covered with a lightproof cover soon after twilight. Loud noises such as radios playing are most disturbing to birds at night. Keep your bird in a room where there is no noise at night, and do make sure the cage cover shuts

What Breed Should I Buy?

out all artificial light. Occasionally, if you want your canary to sing at night, he will do so if you cover his cage in the daytime so that he then gets some rest.

Proper Feeding of Canaries

The seeds and foods mentioned here are obtainable from pet shops and seed merchants. For one bird, buy packaged foods. For many, buy in bulk at pet shops and supply houses. Use the best grades of seeds, rather than the cheapest, for they cost less in the long run, and you will be sure of getting properly cleaned and dust-free seeds and other foods scientifically prepared and compounded to retain their freshness. Be sure to get acquainted with the seed merchant's products at the supply houses that cater especially to bird fanciers. They advertise in bird magazines and will send you their accessory and food catalogs on request. If you are going to keep a lot of birds; it will be best if you buy required seeds separately in large

amounts and mix these yourself. Store seeds in metal containers and keep them in a dry place. Canaries are hard-billed finches, so their staple diet is seeds. Their main seed requirements are canary and rape seeds. Most adult canaries, except Rollers, need a mixture of seventy-five percent canary and twenty-five percent rape seeds. In addition, they need condition seeds. These can consist of equal parts of thistle, steel-cut oats, teazle, dandelion, gold-of-pleasure, and wild seeds that are obtained from grasses, etc. If a small percentage of maw seed and flax are added to the above, a very nicely balanced condition-seed mixture is produced. These, or their equivalent in food value, can be purchased at pet shops or seed dealers, already packaged and at moderate cost if you only possess a few birds. Roller canaries are fed more rape seed than canary, the idea being to keep them less stimulated and their song softer.

Besides the staple canary and rape seeds which your bird requires every day (after all eaten seed husks remaining in the seed cups are blown off), your canary should also receive some of the condition seeds, as before described, in a treat cup. For house canaries, feed this three times weekly. However, breeding canaries need the condition seeds, like the others, every day. Your pet shop can also supply molting and special song foods, some of which contain beneficial cod-liver oil, yeast, iron tonic, and vitamins. Canaries also need green foods, but most people fail to feed their birds these in sufficient quantity and variety. If you live in the city, you can obtain a large assortment of green foods at the big supermarkets. If you reside in the country you can gather most of the required green foods yourself during the spring and summer months.

For canaries, lettuce, endive, watercress, broccoli, escarole, dandelion leaves and roots, clean lawn grass, clover, and wild seeding heads of grasses are all good. A little apple and orange are also beneficial. Contrary to general belief, fresh green foods do not give canaries diarrhea and should be fed every day, especially in spring and summer—all they will eat.

Those who know me personally are well aware that I prefer to feed green foods to canaries more than I do seeds or other foods. But all are necessary. In an outdoor aviary or a large flight cage during the hot summer months, a hundred or more canaries will consume armfuls of greenfoods from noon until nightfall. Lately I've made a new discovery; the feeding of young rape-seed leaves in large amounts will keep most male canaries in full song all during the molt. They seem to prefer this green food to all others. Rape leaves are easy to grow if you have back yard. Just throw left-over seed in a sheltered portion of your yard (mine grow near the kitchen steps), and they keep growing year after year from about April until severe frosts appear.

A half-teaspoon of egg food, described in the chapter on breeding, should be made available once a week to house singers. This can be obtained in prepared form at your seed dealer's or pet shop, or you can make it.

Breeding Canaries

The location of the breeding cage is important: a nice, quiet spot, away from noise and passing people is essential. Never attempt to breed canaries in damp basements.

Canaries for breeding, both males and hens, should always be purchased not later than November or December; then, by the following spring, they will be well accustomed to their new homes and surroundings. Just before you commence breeding, keep the male in one side of the double breeding cage and the hen in the other side, with the solid partition in place so the birds cannot see each other.

The best time to commence breeding is when you see the wild birds in your locality beginning to nest. The temperature of the breeding room should not be over seventy degrees. Males when ready to mate will be singing lustily and will lower their wings and dance about on the perches. The hens, when ready, will have enlarged vents and will also call to their mates frequently. If the weather is warm and settled, and your birds seem ready, remove the solid partition from the breeding cage and place the wire one in its place. If the male begins to feed the hen through the wires, you can take out the partition and leave the birds together. If severe fighting occurs, the birds are not quite ready to begin breeding, so separate them for another week or so. A little mild scrapping, however, does no harm. Beginners are usually too eager to begin, and this causes much grief. Better start late than too early.

The conditioning of the birds prior to breeding is most important. Start feeding the egg or other soft foods about a month before the breeding season starts. One half-teaspoonful per bird per day is sufficient in the beginning, but you can gradually increase the amount given after the first ten days. At this time, feed a lot of green foods also. Condition seeds should be supplied daily, too.

Egg food is made by boiling a fresh egg for twenty minutes. Then it is grated fine or passed through a sieve. Use the white, as well as the yolk. Equal parts of cooked farina and ground

Breeding Canaries

arrowroot biscuit are added, plus a small amount of grated raw carrot to make this mixture crumbly moist. There are good prepared foods on the market, making it unnecessary for you to make the soft food yourself unless you prefer to do it. Some of these prepared foods contain egg, others do not. Anyway, it is advisable to add a little hard-boiled egg to all the prepared foods and to moisten them with grated raw carrot rather than milk or water.

When your pair of canaries seem to be getting along well, you can place a nest pan in the breeding cage. This nest pan must be lined with felt, which should be sewn into the pan. Nesting hair can be given the birds in very small quantities at first. They will usually play with it for awhile, then the hen will begin to build a nest in earnest. Then more nesting hair should be given gradually, enough for the hen to make a nice nest.

After the nest is complete, you can expect the first egg in eight days or longr. When it arrives, remove the egg and keep in a lined box in a fairly cool place.

Place a dummy egg in the nest. Remove the second and third eggs daily, soon after laying. These should be placed in the box with the other egg until next evening, when you remove the three dummy eggs and replace the three real eggs in nest. On the following morning the fourth egg will be laid, and the hen will begin the hatching process, which takes fourteen days. The reason for removing the eggs as laid is so that they will hatch out at about the same time and the chicks will all get an equal start in life.

Sometimes canaries lay only three eggs, and sometimes five, but the normal clutch is four. Eggs are usually laid between 8:00 a.m. and 9:00 a.m. It is advisable to mark down the date the hen begins to sit on the full clutch of eggs. Then you will know how to figure the hatching date. If eggs do not hatch when due, leave them alone for a few days. If the weather is cool, they make take a littler longer to hatch. I think it best if the male is left in with the hen, as he will help a lot with the feeding of the youngsters later on. Keep on

46

Breeding Canaries

feeding soft foods and also a little condition seed while the hen is sitting; and don't forget to feed green food at this time also. When the chicks hatch, give fresh egg food at least three times a day and all the greens the adult birds will eat. Do not disturb the birds more than necessary. Most hens won't feed while you are in the room, especially when the young are newly hatched. As the babies grow, more egg food, condition seeds, and green foods will be necessary. Give the birds all they will eat.

The ideal way to feed birds with fledglings in the nest is as follows: Start feeding egg food soon after daylight, then at noon give a fresh supply of egg food. Also, at noon, start feeding greens and condition seeds. About two hours before darkness sets in, give the final feeding for the day: fresh egg food, more lettuce, and more condition seeds—plenty of it.

Times of feeding should be fairly uniform; the main idea is to have fresh egg food before the birds early in the morning and to keep this available to them, along with the condition seeds and greens, until nightfall.

Sour egg food is a deadly poison to canaries, so remove any spilled or uneaten food before it becomes rancid.

When the youngsters leave the nest, keep on feeding the same as before, right up to the time they can fend for themselves. If the old birds pluck feathers out of the young birds, place the wire partition in the double breeder; remove the nest with young to the other side of the breeding cage, close to the wire partition, and the parent birds will feed the young through the wires. Or you might use a nursery cage, which is a small wire cage that can be hung outside the breeding cage.

The hen will usually want to go to nest again before her offspring can feed themselves. When she does, place another nest pan in her cage. Remove the nest containing the young to the opposite side of the cage, and the male canary will feed them.

When you are sure the young birds can feed themselves, place them in another cage or, preferably, in a larger flight cage. Keep on feeding them egg food,

Breeding Canaries

condition seeds, rape and canary seeds, and greens. It will be some time before they can hull seeds, and they will eat more rape seed in the beginning than the other seeds. Continue feeding soft food right up to the time they finish their first (baby) molt, but when they can hull all of the seeds, the egg food should be given in smaller amounts, twice daily. The first molt of young canaries does not begin until they are about six weeks old, and continues about another six weeks. They shed only their body, head, and neck feathers the first year. Because they retain their flight and tail feathers the first year, they are called "unflighted" canaries.

My own are bred in separate cages in an indoor birdroom. After weaning, they spend several weeks in large ceiling-to-roof flight cages, until they are thoroughly adjusted to a hard-seed diet and strong on the wing. Then if the weather is warm and settled, they are all placed outdoors to fly loose in a large aviary.

After the adult birds have finished nesting, they too join the young birds outdoors. The mixing of young and old in a large outdoor aviary, contrary to the opinions of some fanciers, has proven very satisfactory to me for years. The youngsters soon become as strong as the oldsters and won't submit to any abuse from them.

All my birds molt outdoors and remain outside until the first frost. Then they go indoors and are kept in the large flights for a week or two. After settling down, the young known males are placed in separate cages; the known hens remain in the flight. Old males go into a separate flight. Final sexing begins at this time, and this is determined as quickly as possible, for invariably there are some young birds whose sex has not been determined accurately.

This indoor-and-outdoor method of raising canaries is the ideal way, I believe. This system is also used by our most successful Budgerigar breeders.

A Summer in the Sun

Long ago I learned that a young canary should at least

48

Breeding Canaries

spend the first summer of its life outdoors with ample opportunity to take all the sun baths it desires. Old birds, too, greatly benefit from a summer in the sun. When they can enjoy this every summer after breeding, they usually live to a ripe, old age, rarely needing medicine. It must be remembered, however, that both young and old canaries need ample shade to retire into. Never keep them anywhere unless they have ample and complete shade as well as access to sunshine.

Can One Make a Living Raising Canaries?

I would never advise the novice to drop everything and begin raising canaries as a sole means of earning a livelihood. Like everything else, the successful raising of canaries takes years of experience to learn how to consistently show a profit. While canary raising, in my opinion, is the finest hobby in the world, even for the beginner, it can also be one of the most disappointing hobbies or businesses to those not sufficiently experienced and properly equipped to surmount difficulties that may arise.

To succeed with birds, either for pleasure or for profit, one must have a genuine liking for them; and, strange as it may seem, a person does not really know for certain whether or not he likes birds until he keeps a few of them.

The greatest mistake we all make is thinking that we can learn a business in a very short time. The bird business is just like any other enterprise; those who are making a success of raising and selling birds usually have years of experience in back of them.

Yes, one can make a good living raising birds, if he is content to begin at the bottom and steadily climb upward. There are also splendid opportunities in the bird-food-and-supplies businesses for those who can look ahead and who really will learn to understand what fanciers desire in the ways of bird foods, proper cages, and other supplies and accessories.

Breeding Canaries

Learning the Art of Canary Breeding

First of all, get several of the various books on canary breeding and study them diligently.

By subscribing to one of the periodicals in the field you can read what the authorities have to say about canary breeding and management. Then, you can set your own course of action, being fairly sure you are on the right track. Follow your system with confidence, and keep it up-to-date by constant reading and studying.

I suggest that you pay special attention to the proper feeding of canaries. Learn all you can about this, because more failures, I believe, are due to improper feeding than anything else.

Some writers advise beginners to purchase cheap stock and experiment before getting really good birds. I heartily agree with this in cases where the novice has never read about canaries and is not willing to spend a few weeks studying about them before he starts up.

But, when the beginner has spent considerable time reading up on his subject, perhaps has joined a local bird club and attended a bird show or two, or knows a fellow fancier who will help him out occasionally, I advise him to start out with the very best birds that he can afford. But I suggest he procure free-breeding varieties such as Rollers, Red-factors, American Singers, Borders, Lizards, and Glosters, etc.

Often, to the inexperienced, some of the Yorkshire, Norwich, Scots Fancy, and Dutch Frill canaries may prove to be a little more difficult to breed than the other breeds, so I suggest the beginner get at least a year or two of experience in raising one or more of the other popular breeds before he tackles the more difficult.

However, it would be unkind of me not to give full justice to the breeding qualities of these birds. They can be bred by novices, and I have known of Yorkshires and Norwich that have been better breeders than some of the birds I have listed previously as being easier to breed.

Breeding Canaries

Sexing Young Canaries

Even to a long-established canary breeder this is often quite a problem. Of course, old canaries in full song readily show you immediately and unmistakingly that they are cocks. But one often desires to accurately sex young canaries before you can determine their sex by their song. This is possible only at certain stages of their development. I have read many times about singing hens that were classified as cocks because of their singing ability, and I don't doubt their existence. But, in all the hundreds of canaries that I have bred, I have never had a singing hen that sang in any manner as vigorously or as well as a cock. So, I think that if an old canary has a free and vigorous song, you can safely count him as a male, and you will be correct about ninety-nine and nine-tenths percent of the time.

If your young birds are in flight cages and are five or six months old, catch birds that seem to be singing lustily. Sometimes, you can be almost sure such birds are cocks, but give them this test first. Place them in separate cages with partitions between, so they cannot see other birds. They will be a trifle wild at first but will settle down within a week or two. If they are males, their song will confirm it.

I always make it a rule to never count a young bird as a male until it has been caged a few weeks or long enough to really give it a real chance to sing. Then, if I observe it on several different occasions singing lustily, but not twittering, I class it as a cock. It is quite a tedious job to accurately sex young canaries; but, in my opinion, their song, or lack of it, in time, betrays their sex. But don't class a young canary as a male just because it twitters.

Sexing Canaries in the Nest

When young canaries are in the nest, many young cocks can be recognized at about eight or ten days of age. From my many observations, I would say that

The Health of Your Canary

males even as young as these seem to act in a little more important manner than do the baby hens. For instance, when reaching for food in the nest, young males seem bolder and greedier than the hens. Baby males seem to demand all the food and have that never-mind-anyone-else-but-me attitude.

Another way of sexing in the nest is to watch very closely from a hidden spot in the birdroom: you will notice that the parent hens feed mostly the young cocks, and the parent cocks feed the young hens. As they get older, this is even more and more noticeable.

I strongly urge canary breeders to maintain sexing records of all youngsters in the nest. Note those which seem to be males, and later this will greatly simplify sexing.

Having had no scientific training for the treating of bird ailments and chronic diseases, I do not feel qualified to pose as a bird doctor. My goal has always been to prevent rather than to cure disease. With this in mind, sickness among my own birds and any unnatural deaths have been much below average. Experience has taught me that canaries are not delicate by any means. Long observation and study has proven that while canaries can endure or, I should say, do uncomfortably endure high natural temperatures, such as a few 95-degree days in the summertime, they cannot flourish in the 85-degree or higher temperatures induced by artificial heat in the wintertime. The best winter temperature for them, I have found, is not over 65 degrees, and temperatures almost down to freezing will do no harm if they are accustomed to it in the birdroom.

I am absolutely convinced that many canary ailments are due to high room temperatures in winter, which cause respiratory troubles leading to other illnesses, besides the not-so-

The Health of Your Canary

serious soft molting or unseasonal feather dropping. I am also of the opinion that too many of the so-called miracle drugs are being administered to canaries by well-meaning but unqualified fanciers. These miracle medicines should never be given to well birds with the mistaken idea they will prevent disease; they will have almost the opposite effect. However, I have heard of several remarkable cures made by antibiotics. These drugs were in all cases prescribed by physicians who keep canaries and veterinarians with bird experience.

So, I earnestly urge my readers to exercise great caution in the administration of medicines, especially the "wonder" drugs, to canaries. Never use them for long periods of time, as so many have advised; if you do, you'll have sterile birds or birds which, if they do get sick, will not respond properly to these drugs. To use these drugs intelligently, one must consult a doctor or veterinarian who has studied canary ailments.

Most bird-seed dealers and all pet shops carry a full and complete line of proven bird remedies, together with all the different bird seeds, foods, and most of the cages and breeding accessories mentioned in this book. There are excellent brand-name remedies for nearly every canary ailment; they can be procured when necessary and used as directed. In addition to the remedies, seed dealers and pet shops also carry many canary foods that contain the newer and proven vitamins or antibiotic supplements. However, do not feed canaries an excess of special vitamins or antibiotics. A well-balanced feeding program makes these unnecessary, except in cases of illness. Rather than attempting to compound your own remedies, the writer feels is more satisfactory to buy the best brand-name remedies. In this book he will attempt to prescribe only the more simple remedies that almost everyone has on hand.

Robert Stroud, the famous Bird Man of Alcatraz, wrote a book entitled *Stroud's Digest on the Diseases of Birds* (T.F.H. Publications). It is one of the best books ever written on the

The Health of Your Canary

subject. No serious bird fancier should be without a copy for instant reference.

My Bird Is All Puffed Up

This can be due to many causes, as nearly all canaries puff up their feathers when illness strikes them. Indigestion, caused by wrong or too rich feedings, is a very common canary ailment. The remedy for this is to check up on your feeding methods. A small pinch of epsom salts in the drinking water for a few days will often relieve this condition, if the diet is corrected.

But before you commence to dose your puffed-up bird with medicine or laxatives, it is far better to take the bird gently in your hand and notice its general condition. If it seems light and very thin, this can be due to disease or malnutrition. The best treatment for the latter is to feed soft food containing a few drops of cod-liver oil several times weekly until the bird's condition improves. The droppings of a canary are a good indicator of the bird's health. If they are always watery and loose, there are several good trade-marked remedies. If he is in plump condition and not thin by any means, a simpler diet should be fed, avoiding rich foods, egg foods, etc. Common diarrhea can often be cured by a "starvation diet" for a few days; feed only canary seed and steel-cut oats, and obtain a suitable remedy to put in his drinking water.

In cases of malnutrition, the treatment should be the opposite of this: the bird must be fed a far richer and more varied diet. A healthy canary feels heavy in the hand, and if such a bird becomes suddenly puffed up, the trouble is usually indigestion. If your canary feels very light when you take him in your hand, his feeding must be corrected by giving him richer foods, tonics, and cod-liver oil in minute quantities. A very thin canary may also be suffering from one of the various other diseases and may need an internal antiseptic to kill the germs. Consult your veterinarian about this.

Baldness and Poor Feathers

Baldness and poor feathers are

The Health of Your Canary

sometimes caused by lice and often by wrong feeding. If lice are suspected, first wash the bird. Baldness can be inherited, but it is usually due to the bird having been poorly fed as a youngster. This caused its feathers to be more brittle and weaker than normal, and they have merely worn out. If the bird is fed suitably, feathers will often grow in normally during the next molt. Feed bald birds a little richer diet and ample green foods.

Broken Legs and Wings

In the case of mild leg fractures, it is best to remove all perches, place the food and water in small jar lids close to the bird on the floor of the cage, and leave the bird completely alone. For those with broken legs or wings, the cage must be placed in a very quiet corner of the room, where they won't be frightened or prompted to move because of people passing. If the leg breakage is severe, it may be necessary to make splints from toothpicks. Then, set the bones

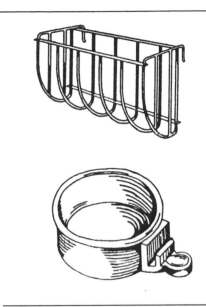

The wire rack (above) can be used to offer greens or nesting material. The round "drawer" (below) is a small cup for soft foods.

in position, apply the splints, and secure these to the leg with thin strips of adhesive tape. Be careful not to wrap these too tightly; otherwise, circulation in the leg will be cut off. Broken legs usually take about ten days to heal.

Some wing breakages can be helped by tying the broken wing in proper, normal position and leaving it tied for about two weeks. If breakage is such that

The Health of Your Canary

Above: Nest pans may be made of wire, plastic, or ceramic. Below: The nursery cage is hung outside, on the wire of the breeding cage.

this cannot be done, just leave the bird alone in a very quiet place where it won't move much. Remove the perches, and place food and water close to him in shallow containers on the floor of the cage.

Colds, Asthma, and Wheezing

Keep the bird a little warmer than usual. Place a very small pinch of epsom salts in the drinking water for two days. After this, a few drops of whiskey in water for a day or two will be beneficial. This usually clears up the common cold. Asthma, especially when it reaches a chronic stage, is

Photographs, pp. 57—64: 57—Variegated Buff Yorkshire. 58—Different breeds: Gloster, Frill, Yorkshire, Border. 59—Cinnamon Border Fancy. 60—Squabbling at bath time. 61—Broken-cap Gold Lizard hen. 62—Green Gloster Hen about to feed her brood. 63—Canaries relish green food. 64—Colorfed Norwich cock.

57

The Health of Your Canary

difficult to cure. Sometimes it is mistaken for tiny, parasitic worms that live in the crop of the bird and crawl up into the throat, causing the bird to wheeze, splutter, and cough. Give him an epsom-salt laxative in drinking water for a few days; then with an eye dropper, put a few drops of ten-percent Argyrol down his throat. Repeat this several times for a few days if necessary.

Soft Molt

Out-of-season dropping of feathers is nearly always caused by sudden changes of temperature. If you keep a canary in a hot, 85-degree room for a few weeks and then suddenly place it in a 65-degree temperature, it will usually go into a partial of soft molt and stop singing. Or, if you keep a canary in a cold room and then suddenly change it to a hot one, the same thing will happen. So, do not change your bird around from room to room where there are great differences of temperature. Always endeavor to keep your bird where the heat is not over seventy degrees, and you will not be troubled with soft molt.

Red Mites and Lice

Mites attack birds only at night. They leave the bird at daylight and crawl into cracks and crevices near the cage or hide on the ends of perches and in corners of the cage, etc. If you suspect their presence, place a white cloth over the cage at night, and, if in the morning you see tiny, red specks crawling around, these are mites full of your bird's blood. They also hide in the daytime in wallpaper and other places close to the cage. They must be kept under control at all times, especially during the summer. If they are present, remove your bird from the cage and thoroughly scald the cage. Spray all around the wallpaper and cracks and possible hiding places close to the cage. Use a spray that is safe for use around birds.

To eradicate lice, purchase a special powder and use as

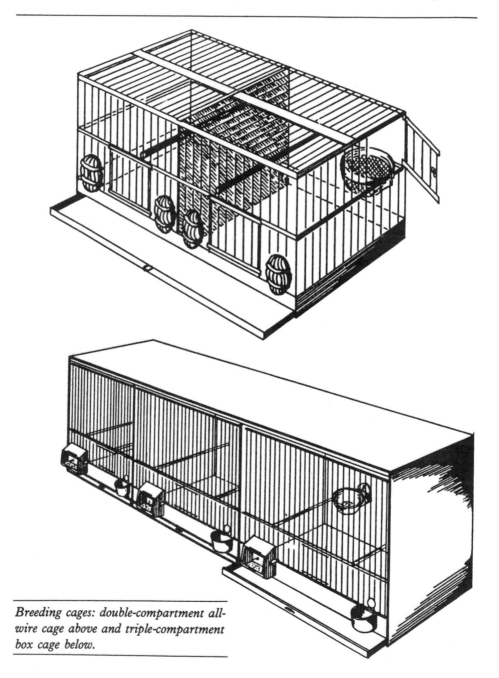

Breeding cages: double-compartment all-wire cage above and triple-compartment box cage below.

directed. Lice on birds are difficult to see with the naked eye, but their presence can be discovered by noting feathers showing marks of having been eaten by the pests. Look for these places on the large wing and tail feathers of the birds. Liquid sprays are sold for this purpose also, and I consider them superior to the powders.

Loss of Song

Canaries, as a general rule, do not sing all the year around. There are certain periods, such as just previous to and during the molting season, when they sing little, if at all. Their song is usually at its best from about October to April. Breeding males do not sing frequently when in the breeding cage with the hen, except when they are "driving her," making love to her.

However, some canaries will not sing during the normal season because of poor feeding or illness. If your bird stops singing for any length of time during the singing season, treat for illness or correct the diet, whichever is the apparent cause.

Scaly Legs and Sore Feet

A tiny mite sometimes lodges in the scales of a canary's legs and sets up an irritation. This causes the scales to enlarge and become ugly. The remedy is to anoint the scaly parts with a medicated petroleum jelly or a special ointment. Apply this for several days; then soak the feet in warm water for a few minutes, and you should be able to gently remove the scales with your fingernail. Be careful to remove only diseased scales. Sore feet are caused by dirty perches, cages, etc. Sometimes they are due to mosquitoes. For this condition, anoint the affected parts with mercurochrome.

Trimming Claws and Beaks

Hold the bird's feet in a strong light and you will see the red blood vessels which extend from the toes into the claws. Using sharp nail scissors, trim the claws about an eighth of an inch away from these vessels. Sometimes a canary's upper mandible grows too long and hangs over the lower. Simply trim off this overhang.

Fits in Canaries

Feeding stale egg food or too warm a temperature will cause fits, especially in young canaries. Loud noises close to the bird, or the presence of a cat staring at the bird, are two more reasons for this distressing condition.

If the fit is severe and the bird flops helplessly to the floor of the cage, gently take it in your hand and place the head in cold water for a second or two, keeping the beak and nostrils out of the water. This will sometimes bring the canary around. Keep the bird extra quiet for a few days.

The Annual Molt

This is the time when a lot of improperly fed and poorly managed canaries expire. The natural molting season usually starts in July and extends until October. Not all birds begin molting at the same time—some are earlier or later than others. The complete molt usually takes six weeks or a little longer. Male canaries sing little when shedding their feathers.

In the early stages of the molt, birds present a very drowsy appearance; they seem dopey and sleepy in the daytime. Then, a few tail feathers fall out, and the molt is underway. Nature has endowed birds with the ability to molt gradually; they lose only a few feathers at a time, so that they will not lose their protective power of flight.

Molting canaries need a richer diet to see them through this trying time and should be fed during this period as prescribed in the chapter on feeding canaries for conditioning and breeding. They should be given egg food daily, molting foods, and a lot of green food. If these feeding suggestions are carried out, your canary will molt out perfectly and beautifully.

Egg Binding

Egg binding is usually caused by mating birds too early in the season or when the hen is too young to breed. Canaries should be at least ten months old before they are mated. The best cure is to place the hen in a hospital cage or box warmed with an electric light bulb at a temperature of about 80 degrees for one hour; then if the egg is not passed, raise temperature to 95 degrees Fahrenheit, but not higher. If a few drops of olive oil from the end of a toothpick are dropped into the vent (without touching it with the toothpick), a lubricating action will take place and will make the passing of the egg much easier for the hen. Sometimes it is advisable to gently massage the abdomen of the hen to gently push the egg outward. This action must be sensitive and gentle; too much force may break the egg, which is often fatal to the hen.

Another method, if no hospital cage is available, is to place hot water in a milk bottle, cover the opening of the bottle with a light cloth, and gently steam the vent of the hen, holding her a reasonable distance away so there is no danger of scalding or further irritating the delicate membranes of the vent.

When the egg is passed, a tiny drop of belladonna gently dropped into the swollen vent opening will cause it to close to normal position.

The Nonfeeding Hen

I am going to discuss the nonfeeding hen in detail because all canary breeders suffer with this problem every breeding season. In some cases nothing can be done, but I have found that the suggestions below will often help.

When the chicks hatch, the hens do not begin feeding them until the babies are several hours old, and often they are not fed for a longer period than this. Nature has supplied the new-born chicks with sufficient nutriment to last them for about eight hours or longer after they emerge from the shells.

Often the novice, noticing that the chicks have hatched and that the mother bird does not rush off the nest and immediately begin feeding, gets panicky and starts interfering with the nest. Then

The Health of Your Canary

the hen gets panicky too, and when the time arrives for her to begin feeding, she is too upset and nervous to do the job right. I have found that interfering and peeking into the nest right after the chicks are born is the greatest cause of hens not feeding properly.

The next period when nonfeeding is likely to occur is when the chicks are about eight days old, or just about the time when the hen stops cleaning out the nest. If the mother bird fed well up to this time, nonfeeding is usually due to her not feeling well—a sort of stomach upset, as it were. The best remedy I know of at this point is to place a small pinch of epsom salts in drinking water for a day, and also to give the bird plenty of green lettuce, and bread and milk if she will eat it. The idea is to help clean out her system, and when this done, she will usually begin feeding again.

If a hen, before and during breeding, has shown a liking for the soft food you use and then with chicks in the nest suddenly stops eating and feeding it, immediately give her an epsom-salt or bread-and-milk laxative and supply lots of *green* lettuce. Some hens prefer head lettuce to the green-leaf variety, but feed only the crisp, outer green leaves.

Lettuce has performed miracles in my bird room; I have had hens that will feed little else and raise large, healthy birds too. However, with such hens I always feed lots of condition seeds such as thistle, teazle, dandelion, etc. These birds are also given liberal supplies of steel-cut oats, besides the staple canary and rape seeds.

The Sweating Hen

This condition is noticeable when the hen with chicks in the nest appears to have a very wet breast. It is caused by the chicks' excreta being too liquid; they have diarrhea. Change the nest lining several times daily and give the hen a small pinch of epsom salts in the drinking water for a day. Then, after skipping one day, add a tiny pinch of table salt to the drinking water for one day only. Give the hen

Cages and Accessories

bread and milk also, if she will eat it. You can sprinkle this with maw seed. Do not stop the feeding of lettuce. Bacteria cause this condition, not greens.

The Yorkshire is one of the larger breeds, so it requires more spacious accommodations.

There are literally dozens of different designs in breeding cages. I have seen them made out of packing crates, orange boxes, and other crude things. It is true that prize birds may be raised successfully in these contraptions, but if your cages are well made, present a good appearance, and are of uniform design, you will get much more pleasure when viewing them. And they will, if correctly designed, be a lot easier to clean and will make caring for your birds much easier.

I suggest you have single, double, and triple-compartment breeding cages of the box type, and only double-compartment cages of all-wire construction.

All-Wire and Box Cages

Breeding cages consist of two general styles: all-wire for the smaller breeds such as Red-factors, American Singers, Rollers, etc., and the larger box cages for Yorkshires, Borders, and Norwich.

The smaller all-wire cages can be obtained at very reasonable

Cages and Accessories

cost. Some of the latest models have hinged tops that swing open, making interior cleaning easier. Also, these cages can be folded flat for easy storage when not in use. Some have two sets of seed and water cups, which is handy; soiled ones can be sterilized while clean ones are in use.

This cage can be divided into two compartments, using either a solid metal or a wire partition. These slide into position from the top or the front of the cage. Three perches on each side are ample for this size cage. During the breeding season, the male can be placed in one compartment, the female in the other; and, at first, the solid panel can be placed in position so the birds cannot see each other. Later, the wire partition can be inserted in the cage, and, if the birds are ready to begin nesting, the male will feed the hen through the wires.

Use this double-compartment breeding cage for one pair of birds only. Have at least one cage for each pair of canaries you are going to breed. I mention this because some breeders cage two hens in one of these breeders, with the solid panel dividing the cages into two sections. Then they alternately run the males in with these hens until the nests are built and the eggs are laid. The males are then removed, and the hens are left to incubate the eggs and to rear the youngsters by themselves.

These cages are far too small and were not designed to accommodate two hens. It is far better to allow a whole cage for proper exercise. Remember that when the chicks hatch and are old enough to leave the nest, they need plenty of room to move about before they are old enough to be taken from their parents and placed in flight cages.

In the event that either of the parent birds should begin to pluck feathers out of the young birds, the young can be placed in the other half of the cage with the wire partition set in place to separate the adult birds from their offspring. The fledglings will then be fed through the wire partition by the parent birds. And, if the hen has gone to nest again, the feeding of the youngests will be undertaken by the male if he has been left in with the hen. In my opinion, and because most male canaries are good feeders, they always should be left in with the hens, even though most hens will rear their broods if left alone.

The only advantage in removing the male after his hen has gone to nest is in cases where he is being used with another hen or hens. Then he should be always removed from the hens at the proper time: when the eggs have been fertilized and the hen has begun sitting.

Usually one copulation will fertilize all the eggs, which are laid at daily intervals. But if you want to be doubly sure that proper fertilization has taken place, leave the male with the hen until the third egg has been laid. If he has been left in with her until the whole clutch has been laid and incubation started, the male can generally be removed from that particular mate without disturbing her. In a few cases, hens will desert their nests if their mates are removed at the wrong time.

When the hen goes to nest for the second time, usually a little before the previous brood is quite ready to care for itself, the spare half of the all-wire double breeding cage makes an ideal spot in which to place the youngsters for a few days, until you are certain they can eat without assistance from the male and are sufficiently advanced for removal to the flight cage.

All-Wire Cages Are Easy to Clean

The all-wire cages, especially when one has a lot of birds, are probably the easiest of all cages to clean and keep in a sanitary condition. They can be totally submerged occasionally in hot water to which a little detergent or disinfectant has been added and thus kept lice- and germ-free. The sliding trays, which pull out from the front, can be covered with newspaper and changed when needed in a few minutes' time. These cages also require a minimum of space, as they can be stacked on shelves one upon the other.

Cages and Accessories

Seed and Water Cups

The food receptacles for these cages consist of two seed cups and two water cups for each double breeder. When the male is running with the hen, canary seed can be placed in one seed cup, rape in the other, and the two water cups allow plenty for drinking.

The grit should be placed in one of those little round glasses, called egg cups, and suspended on the bars of cages above the floor with the wire holders that can be obtained to fit them.

Egg food can be fed in another one of these glass cups, also suspended off the floor of cage. Then, when it's cage-cleaning time and the papers in the trays need changing, there is nothing on the floor of the cages to remove before pulling out the trays. Grit and soft food suspended in vessels above the cage floors are less liable to become contaminated by the birds' droppings.

If you keep the smaller canary breeds, you will find the all-wire breeding cages the best in the long run, but no canary should be kept in a small cage all of the time. They should molt and be kept in large flight cages except when breeding or when it is necessary to cage them for some other reason.

Box Cages Best for Type Birds

Box cages consist of a square box with a wire front and a sliding drawer that pulls out from the front for cleaning purposes. Box cages can be single, double, triple, or even larger; but the more compartments one of these box cages has, the more difficult it is to handle, especially when enamelling the inside or disinfecting it.

Norwich, Yorkshire, Border Fancy, and the other large type breeds require this style of cage, which is far larger than the all-wire breeding cages previously described. The ideal size for a single-unit box cage is about eighteen inches long, eleven inches deep, and eighteen inches high. If you decide on a double- or triple-compartment box cage,

Cages and Accessories

the overall size will be correspondingly larger.

The wire fronts on these cages are easily removed, and the sliding doors in front are large enough so that nest pans can be placed inside and taken out for inspection and cleaning purposes readily.

Box breeding cages look most attractive if enamelled light blue on the wood section of the front and on the entire inside of the cage; the sides, top, and base should be black. The best color for the wire fronts of canary breeding cages is jet black. Be certain that enamel for canary cages does not contain lead, as wire fronts and interiors can poison any birds that peck at paint containing lead.

Yellow, red-orange, or other colored canaries observed through jet-black wire fronts are easier to see than if the wires are the natural chrome color.

Advantages of Single, Double and Triple Box Cages

The single box cage is ideal for caging male type birds, which should be kept one to a cage. This size cage is also used as a breeding cage, being large enough for one pair of birds. A cage of this size is also easy to handle.

The two-compartment box cage is best when made with a sliding partition of wood, which pulls in and out from the front of the cage. This partition should be made deep enough to extend outward in front of cage about two inches, so that the birds in each cage cannot see each other. A small interior transfer door is convenient.

It is nice too, to have a removable wire partition to fit the double box cage. Then this all-equipped cage can be used as a double stock cage; a single breeding or double breeding cage; a combined single-breeding and nursery cage (when the wire partition is in place); or as a pre-mating cage (when it is advisable to place the male in one section, the hen in the other, for the time necessary for them to become acquainted with each other, before the wire partition is withdrawn).

The canary fancier who

Cages and Accessories

possesses attractive and well-made cages will find that they not only help the appearance of the bird room but also make it much easier for him to clean the cages and to feed and care for the birds. Cages with punch-bar fronts are far superior to those with the makeshift hardware-cloth fronts. Hardware cloth should be used only in large flight cages and outside aviaries.

The triple-compartment box cage has two removable partitions of wood, and can also have two punch-bar wire partitions which can be used when the wooden ones are not in place.

This cage may be used as three separate caging units; three breeding cages; or in the many other combinations suggested for double breeding cages. With both wood and wire partitions, many different and highly useful combinations are possible, making it a most valuable cage. It can also be used when one male is being used with two hens, the male's quarters being the center section. The three-compartment cage also makes a good small flight cage for type

birds if the partitions are removed. Several birds can be run together and will get a moderate amount of exercise. But, on the whole, I think it best to use a larger flight cage for canaries when they are not breeding, one big enough for them to really fly around in.

Feeding Utensils and Perches

It is best to use plastic or metal seed hoppers for all the box cages. The best water containers I have found for box cages are made of thick plastic. These hold a more-than-usual supply of water, which is good for large type birds, especially when breeding. Being of heavy construction, these larger-size drinkers will not warp when being sterilized, are practically unbreakable, and will not contaminate anythig administered to canaries.

The perches required for type birds are larger in diameter than those for the smaller breeds, and the ideal perch is oval rather than round. It should measure five-eighths of an inch by three-eighths of an inch in diameter. Perches should always be made of very soft wood; hard wood is rather severe on a canary's feet, often causing corns and sores.

Three perches are usually used in each box cage. The two upper ones should be made long enough to extend out through the wire front and between the wires about an inch so they can be grasped from the outside of cage for cleaning.

An Easy Way to Clean Perches

While all perches should be immersed in boiling water containing a suitable disinfectant at least once a week, it is often necessary to scrape them more frequently. If you take a piece of suitable metal and cut half-circle and half-oval slots that are a trifle larger in diameter than your round and oval perches, you will have a dandy perch scraper. The perch fits into the slot, and the scraper is merely run forward and backward over the perches, removing excreta much easier than a wire brush will. Steel-wool pads are also useful in the bird room for scraping dirt off perches and from the interior backs and sides of box cages.

Bird-Room Utensils

Type birds, of course, require a larger nesting receptacle than the small wire nest pans usually used for the other breeds.

The newest, and that which many leading fanciers consider the best, type of nest pan for large canaries is made of heavy plastic. Unlike the old-style pottery ones, it is unbreakable and, like the plastic drinker, can be sterilized without distorting its shape. This nest pan requires no separate wire holder to suspend it from the back or sides of the box cage. All it needs is a small hook to hold it firmly in the breeding cage.

An egg crusher, used when making egg food, is also made of plastic and is useful for fanciers who only keep a few birds.

Round egg-food drawers fit under the sliding wire doors of box cages and are held firmly in position by the bottom of the

Cages and Accessories

door, which fits into a groove on the drawer when the door is down and closed. The newest ones are made of plastic and, being much larger than the round glass cups usually used in all-wire cages, are ideal for use with the larger breeds in box cages. Type birds, of course, consume more soft food than the smaller breeds, so their feeding utensils should always be amply large.

Many fanciers have trouble getting their canaries to take a bath in one of the outside bird baths. The birds seem afraid of them. But if a bird is introduced to one of these outside baths when still very young, the canary will soon get used to it. However, I have found that older birds that shy at these baths will often enter one if a convenient perch is placed inside, just about at the level of the water. They will hop onto this perch, look around a bit, then dunk their heads in the water. Soon, they will jump right in and take a good bath.

The author has been raising canaries for decades. He fully realizes that some of the subjects and methods he has suggested in this book may be contradictory to some published in other books and magazines, but he wishes to point out that the ideas described here have been successful for him, and that we should remember there are often more ways than one of doing things successfully. The author's methods have been primarily learned from his long practical experience.

Seed hoppers discourage birds from scattering seed.

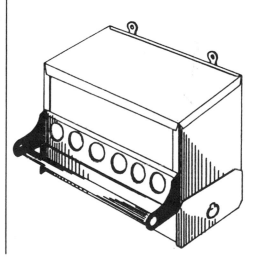

Canaries are bred to emphasize certain characteristics, often at the expense of others. A canary bred for song (above) will likely not have the excellence of form found in a breed that stresses conformation, like the Border (below).

Further Reading

Here are other good books about canaries that will help you to learn about your birds and enjoy them more.

ENCYCLOPEDIA OF CANARIES
By G.T. Dodwell
ISBN 0-87666-952-6
TFH H-967

For the newcomer to the canary fancy. Covers early fanciers, breeding systems, heredity and environment, types of exhibition, birdrooms, and cage fittings. Ages 15 years and older.
Contents: History. Housing And Equipment. Feeding And General Management. Breeding—Practical. Breeding—Theory. Molting. Exhibiting. Diseases And Parasites. Color And Markings. The Border Fancy. The Yorkshire. The Norwich. The Gloster Fancy. The Lizard. Other Varieties Of British Origin. Varieties From Continental Europe. Canaries In North America. The Red Factor And Other New Colors. The Roller.
Hard cover, 5½ x 8", 281 pages
28 black and white photos, 48 color photos

HANDBOOK OF CANARIES
By Dr. Matthew M. Vriends
ISBN 0-87666-876-7
TFH H-994

Handbook of Canaries is an indispensable reference work for everyone interested in these beautiful and interesting birds, from champion breeders and experienced fanciers to those who simply keep a pet canary. Highlighted with many, many full-color photos of good birds.
Contents: Introduction. A Little History.

Housing Canaries in Cages and Aviaries. The Care and Feeding of the Canary. A Little Ornithology. Keeping Canaries. Diseases, Accidents, and Parasites. Breeding Canaries. Color Canaries. Form and Posture Canaries.
Hard cover, 320 pages 5½ x 8"
86 full-color photos, 160 black and white photos, 2 line drawings

THE TFH BOOK OF CANARIES
ISBN 0-87666-819-8
TFH HP-010

The TFH Book of Canaries thoroughly explores the latest methods of health care, housing, feeding and breeding. In addition, the history of the canary is discussed and a full description of various canary types given. An excellent eye-opener for the novice bird-keeper and a valuable key for the experienced canary lover.
Hard cover, 8½ x 11", 80 pages

DISEASES OF CANARIES
By Robert Stroud [The Birdman
   of Alcatraz]
ISBN 0-87666-436-2
TFH PS-640

This book discusses everything of interest to canary keepers who want to maintain their birds' good health, from a complete discussion of good feeding programs and canaries' anatomy through detailed treatments of every significant canary injury and disease. Not up to date, but authoritative and compellingly interesting to anyone interested in canaries.
Hard cover, 5½ x 8", 239 pages